The Nature Kid's Guide to DUCKS

DAVID ANDERSON

LP Media Inc. Publishing
Text copyright © 2026 by LP Media Inc.
All rights reserved.

For information address LP Media Inc. Publishing,
30012 Variolite St NW, Princeton MN 55371
www.lpmedia.org

Publication Data

Ducks
The Nature Kid's Guide to Ducks — First edition.

Summary: "Learn all about Ducks, the Nature Kid Way"
— Provided by publisher.

ISBN: 979-8-89818-184-0

[1. Ducks – Non-Fiction] I. Title.

Title: The Nature Kid's Guide to Ducks

CONTENTS

DISCOVERING DUCKS

Ducks can sleep with one eye open! Half their brain stays awake to watch for danger.

4

Quack! A mallard duck paddles across a shiny pond.

Ducks are some of the most amazing birds on the planet, and they are all around us! But there is so much more to them than most people realize.

Ducks are built perfectly for life in the water. Their flat bills can feel food hiding in muddy water. Its webbed feet work like paddles, pushing it along fast and smooth. Even its feathers are waterproof. Water just rolls right off!

There are more than 120 kinds of ducks in the world. Some are plain brown. Others flash bright green or deep blue. But no matter the color, shape, or size, every single duck is hiding some amazing secrets!

FEATHER SECRETS

Some ducks have more than 14,000 feathers covering their body!

Swoosh! A duck shakes water off its back in a flash.

Duck feathers do more than look pretty. Each feather has a coating of oil. This oil keeps water out and keeps the duck dry, even after hours of swimming.

Ducks spread oil on their feathers with their bills. This is called **preening**. They rub and smooth each feather one by one. A duck may spend hours preening every day.

Under the top feathers, ducks have soft, fluffy **down**. Down traps warm air close to the body. It works like a cozy blanket, keeping ducks warm even in icy water.

TRIPLE TALENTS

Ducks can hold their breath underwater for up to one minute!

Splash! A duck slips under the water without a sound.

Ducks can swim, fly, and dive. Three cool talents in one bird! Webbed feet help them swim by pushing them through the water like boat paddles.

Ducks are strong fliers, too. Some fly thousands of miles each year. Their wings beat fast and never seem to tire. Some ducks can reach speeds of 50 miles per hour!

Other ducks are amazing divers. Tufted ducks can plunge more than 40 feet deep. They pop back up with food in their bills, ready for another dive.

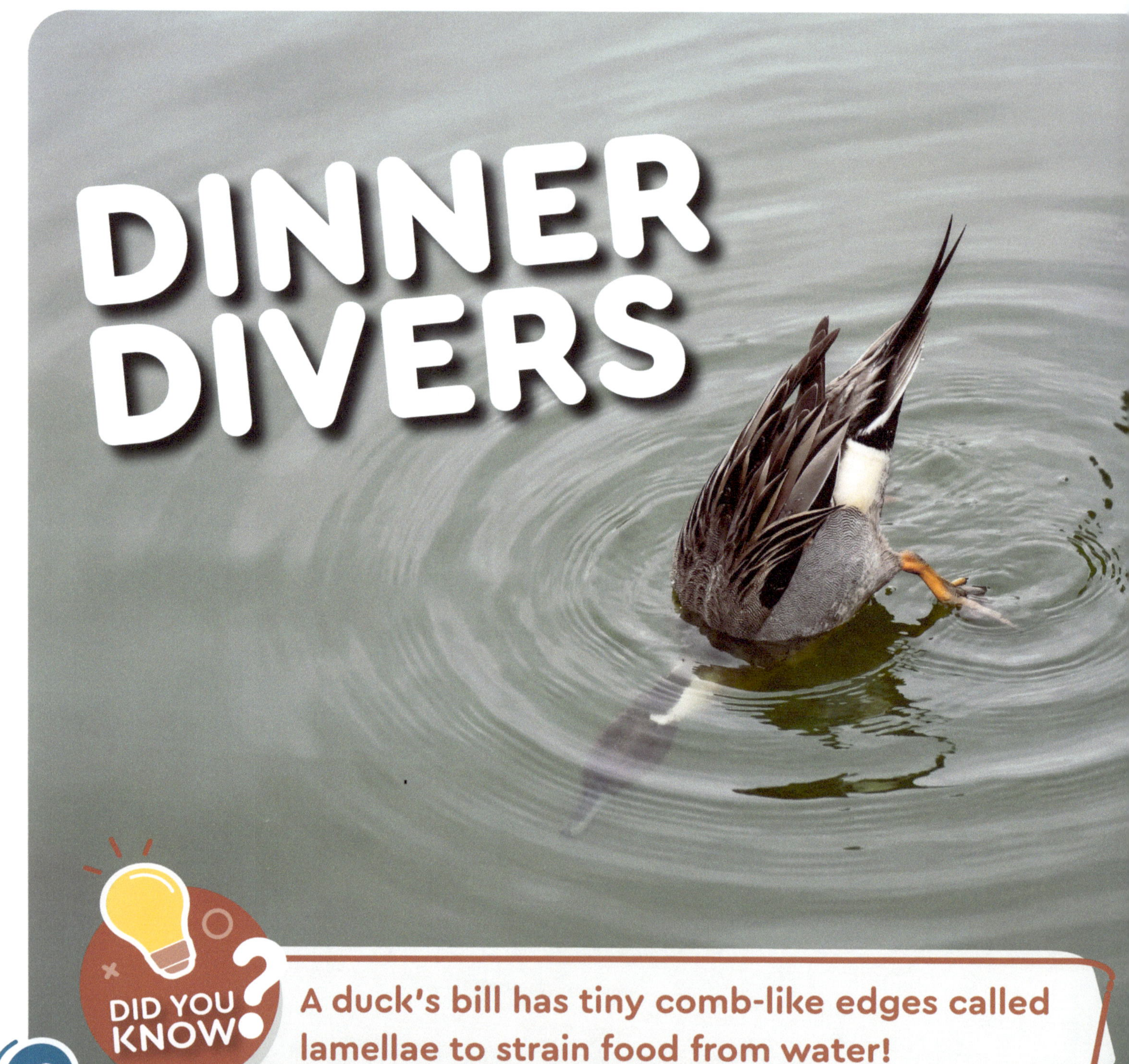

DINNER DIVERS

Slurp! A duck tips its head under and grabs a tasty snack.

Ducks eat many different things. Some munch on plants, seeds, and grain. Others catch bugs, snails, and small fish.

Some ducks tip forward in the water to eat. Only their tails stick up! These ducks are called **dabbling** ducks. Northern pintails eat this way, bobbing up and down all day long.

Other ducks dive all the way under to find food. They use their flat bills to scoop and filter what they find. A duck's bill can sort tiny food from mud in seconds.

DAZZLING DRAKES

Honk! A male duck puffs up and bobs his shiny green head.

Male ducks are called **drakes**. In spring, drakes try to win a mate. They bob their heads, splash water, and call out loud. The showiest drake often wins!

Drakes have bright feathers to catch a female's eye. Mallard drakes have shiny green heads that gleam in the sun. The females are brown, which helps them hide on their nests.

After mating, the female builds a nest near water. She tucks it between tall grasses or under bushes. Then she lays about ten eggs and keeps them warm for a month.

MIGRATION MAGIC

Some ducks migrate at night, using the stars to find their way through the dark sky.

Whoosh! A flock of ducks take off and fill the autumn sky.

When the seasons change, many ducks pack up and go. They fly south to find warm water and plenty of food. When spring returns, they turn around and head back north to nest.

Some ducks travel incredible distances. Northern pintails fly all the way from Alaska to Hawaii, crossing more than 2,000 miles of open ocean without a single place to stop and rest. That is one of the longest flights of any duck in the world!

Ducks do not make that journey alone. They fly together in a V shape, which saves energy. The duck up front cuts through the wind, and the others glide along in its path.

MARVELOUS MALLARDS

Nearly all farm ducks are related to wild mallards that people tamed over 2,000 years ago!

Quack! A mallard calls out from the edge of a still pond.

Mallards live on six of the seven continents. You will not find them in Antarctica! They feel at home near ponds, rivers, and even city parks.

A mallard drake has a yellow bill and one curly tail feather. Both males and females have a blue wing patch called a speculum. This bright spot flashes when they fly.

After breeding season, male mallards do something strange. They shed their bright green feathers and grow dull brown ones instead, making them look almost exactly like females. It is like the male duck puts on a disguise every summer!

LEAPING DUCKLINGS

Wood ducklings are just one day old when they jump from the nest—and they never get hurt!

Plop! A tiny wood duckling leaps from its nest high in a tree.

Wood ducks nest in tree holes, sometimes 50 feet up. That is as high as a five-story building! When the babies hatch, they must jump to the ground. They bounce and land safely on soft leaves below.

Wood duck drakes are very colorful. They have red eyes, green heads, and white stripes. Many people think they are the prettiest duck in North America.

These ducks live near ponds and swamps with lots of trees. They use their sharp claws to perch on branches, something most ducks cannot do.

MAGNIFICENT MANDARINS

Flap! A mandarin duck lands with a flash of orange and purple.

Mandarin ducks come from East Asia, where they live along rivers and lakes lined with trees. In China and Japan, people see them as a sign of love and loyalty.

It is easy to see why. The male has bright orange, purple, and green feathers that glow like a painting. Two large sail-shaped feathers fan out from his sides. No other duck on Earth looks anything like him!

Mandarin ducks have also spread to new places. Some now live wild in England and California, brought there by people long ago. They found their new homes just fine and never left.

COLD PROOF

FUN FACT!
A single eider down blanket may need feathers from about 60 nests—and can cost thousands of dollars!

Brrrr! A king eider bobs in icy Arctic water without a shiver.

Eider ducks live in cold, northern seas. They are large and tough. Icy cold water does not bother them one bit!

Eider down is super soft and warm. The mother plucks it from her own chest to line the nest. People have used eider down in cozy blankets for hundreds of years. It is one of the warmest materials on Earth.

These ducks dive to eat mussels and clams on the sea floor. They swallow the shells whole! Strong stomachs crush the shells inside their bodies.

TWISTING TEALS
DID YOU KNOW?
A flock of teals can change direction in the air all at once, like a single flying creature!
24

Zip! A pair of green-winged teals twist through the air like little jets.

Teals are some of the smallest ducks. Quick and nimble! They can twist, turn, and dodge trees at top speed.

Green-winged teals have a patch of green on their heads and a bright green stripe on each wing. These small ducks weigh only about 12 ounces. That is less than a can of soup!

Teals live in marshes and shallow ponds. They use their small bills to pick seeds and tiny bugs from the water. When danger comes, they burst into the air in a flash.

PINTAIL PERFECTION

Swish! A pintail glides across the lake with its long tail held high.

Northern pintails are tall and graceful ducks. The drake has a chocolate brown head with a white stripe running up his neck. His two long tail feathers give this duck its name.

Pintails are one of the first ducks to nest each spring. They lay their eggs on the ground in short grass. The nest is just a small dip in the earth, lined with soft down.

Northern pintails are built for speed. They **migrate** at night, flying at nearly 50 miles per hour in the dark! When they are ready to land, they zig-zag down from high in the sky like a falling leaf before leveling off at the last second.

HARLEQUIN HUNTERS
FUN FACT!
Harlequin ducks can walk along the bottom of fast-moving streams, gripping rocks with their strong feet!

Crash! A harlequin duck rides huge waves smashing on the rocks.

Harlequin ducks love rough water. They swim in rocky streams and crashing ocean waves. Most ducks would stay far away!

These ducks are named for their bold markings. Drakes have dark blue feathers with white spots and streaks. The pattern looks like a clown's painted face, which is what harlequin means.

Harlequin ducks dive to find food among the rocks. They eat crabs, snails, and small sea creatures. Strong currents do not slow them down. These tough ducks thrive where others cannot survive.

MUSCOVY MISFITS
FUN FACT!
Muscovy ducks are the only domestic ducks not related to mallards!
30

Hiss! A big muscovy duck fluffs up and guards its favorite spot.

Muscovy ducks are not like other ducks. They are big and heavy, weighing up to 15 pounds. They have bumpy red skin on their faces. Instead of quacking, they hiss and wag their tails!

These ducks come from Central and South America. Wild muscovies roost in trees at night. They grip branches with their strong clawed feet, safe from predators below.

Muscovies have been kept on farms for hundreds of years. They are calm and friendly. Many people around the world raise them for eggs and meat.

RAPIDS RIDER

DID YOU KNOW?

Torrent ducks can swim in water so powerful it would knock a grown person off their feet!

Roar! A torrent duck paddles through wild, rushing rapids.

Torrent ducks live in the mountains of South America. They make their homes along fast, rocky rivers in the Andes. Foamy rapids are no problem for these brave birds!

These ducks have stiff tails that help them steer in strong currents. Their feet have extra-strong claws to grip slippery rocks. They can hold their place in water that would sweep other birds away.

Torrent ducks eat tiny water bugs called larvae. They pick them off rocks while the river rushes past. Each pair of ducks guards its own stretch of river and chases away intruders.

DUCKS EVERYWHERE

Plop! A pink-eared duck lands gently on a pond.

Ducks live in almost every part of the world. Some swim in hot jungle rivers. Others float on cold Arctic seas. Wherever there is water, you might find ducks!

Different places have different ducks. Steamer ducks live along the coast of South America. Pink-eared ducks paddle in Australia. Each kind fits its home just right.

Some ducks love hot places. Others prefer icy lakes. From tropical swamps to frozen shores, ducks have found a way to thrive everywhere.

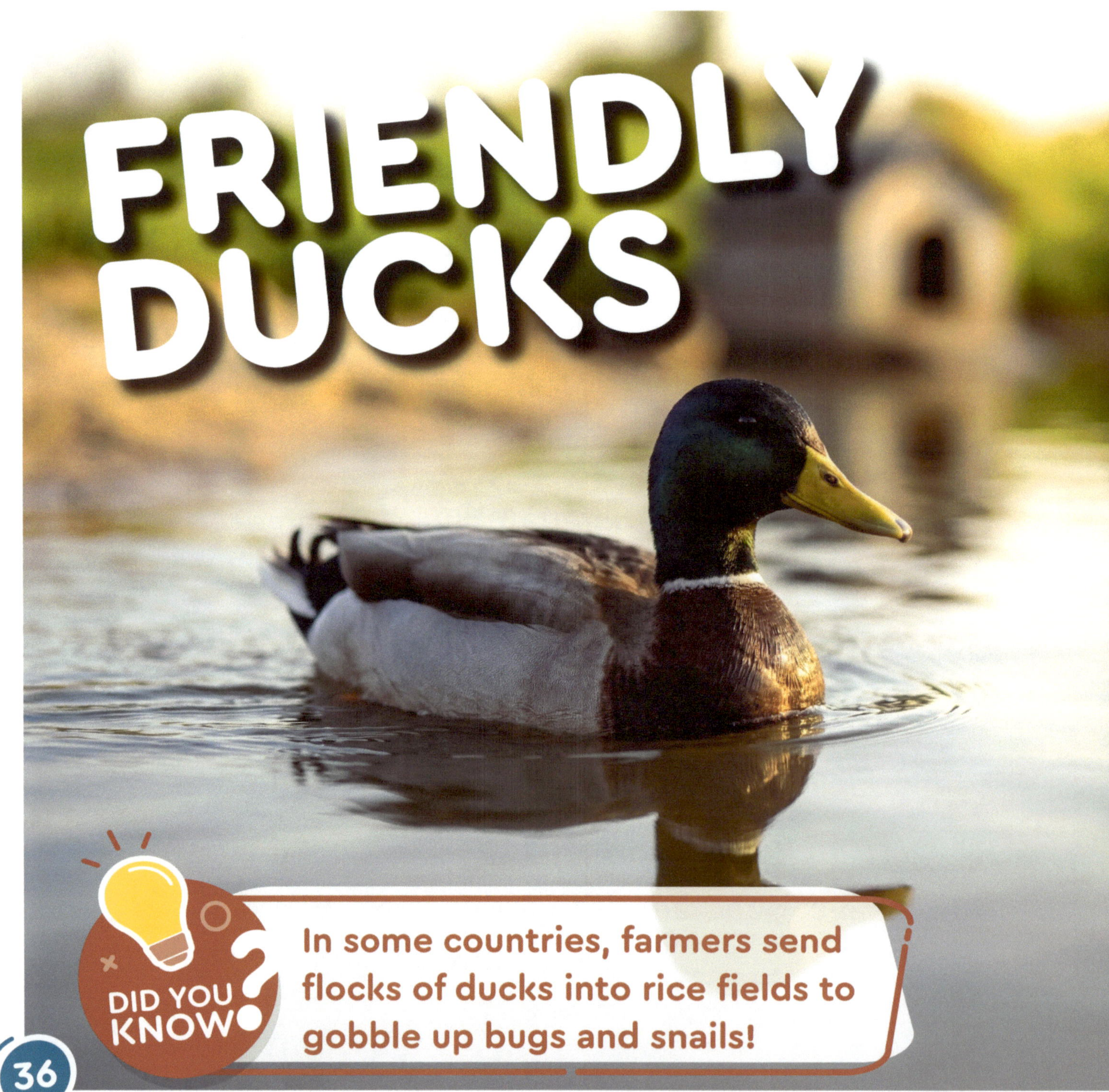

FRIENDLY DUCKS

Woosh! A mallard paddles in a pond at the park.

People and ducks have been friends for a long time. Ducks were some of the first birds to be domesticated. That was over 4,000 years ago in China!

Today, ducks still help people in many ways. Their soft feathers fill warm coats and pillows. Their eggs make tasty foods around the world. Some farmers even use ducks to eat pests like snails.

Ducks also need our help. When we care for wetlands, we help ducks. Clean ponds and rivers give them safe places to live, raise their young, and find food.

DUCK DIVERSITY

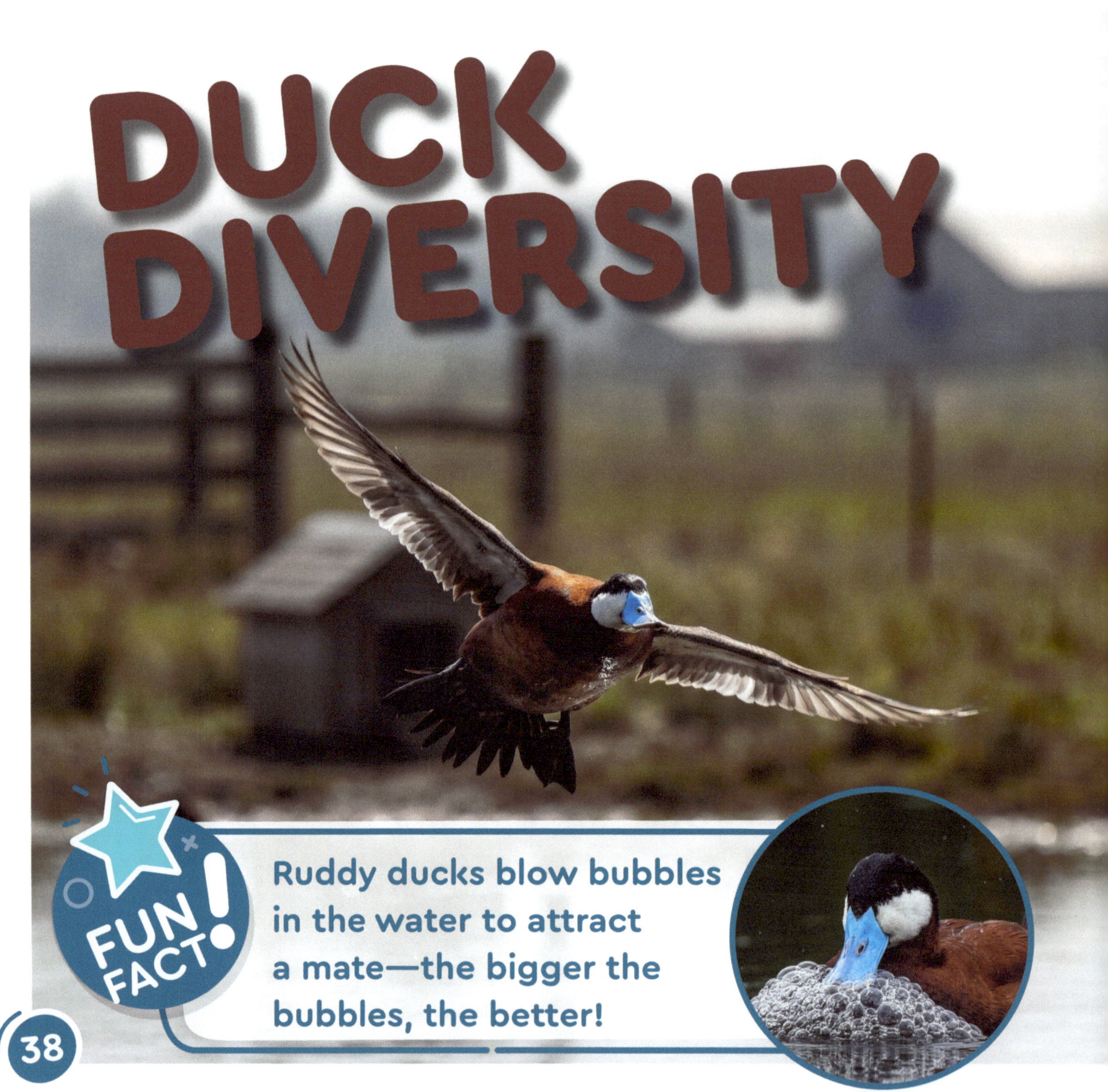

38

Whirr! Wings spread wide as a ruddy duck swoops in to land.

From tiny teals to big muscovies, ducks come in all shapes and sizes. Some are plain brown. Others glow with green, blue, and orange. Every single one has something amazing to discover.

Ruddy ducks are small but bold. The males turn bright reddish brown in spring. They puff up their sky-blue bills and splash around to show off for females.

Now you know what to look for! Head to any pond, lake, or river and see how many different ducks you can spot. The more you watch, the more you will see!

GLOSSARY

preening
Cleaning and oiling feathers using the bill

down
Soft, fluffy feathers close to a bird's body that keep it warm

drake
A male duck

dabbling
Tipping forward in water to eat food just under the surface

migrate
To travel far away to find food or warmer weather